Shadow puppets
for children

Erika Zimmermann

Shadow puppets
for children

Floris Books

Translated by Donald Maclean

First published in German under the title
Wir spielen Schattentheater
by Verlag Freies Geistesleben, Stuttgart 1979.
First published in English in 1983 by Floris Books
Second edition 1990

British Library CIP Data

Zimmermann, Erika
Shadow puppets for children
1. Shadow pantomimes and plays — Juvenile literature
2. Puppet theatres — Juvenile literature
I. Title
791.5'3   PN1979.S5

ISBN 0-86315-108-6

Printed in Great Britain
by BPCC Hazell Books   , Aylesbury, Bucks

Contents

Foreword

'Let's act it. You be the giant, I'll be the tailor and all you can be the flies I'm going to swot.'

Isn't this the healthy outcome of a well-told story? Once the imagination is captured, children want to *do*, to be active; they become so absorbed in their play that our time and space no longer exists.

Children's play is as serious for them as work is to the adult; that absorption in play trains the healthy faculty of concentration so essential for satisfaction in life.

It is self-created play which cultivates the qualities necessary for soul satisfaction in work, not so called 'learning toys'. An understanding of this basic need of childhood has led to adventure playgrounds where the children's phantasy and ingenuity are allowed full range.

The 'box' in our living-rooms stultifies and immobilizes their action, making the 'seeing' of the eye passive. What better remedy for this than to construct a 'box' of their own where the characters come out of their own creative imagination or out of the fairy tales that provided spiritual nourishment down the centuries?

This small book helps us to do just this. The everyday activities beloved of the youngest in the family can be seen in action. Children love to see the reflection of their own experiences. There are fairy stories to nourish their imagination, or they can write their own plays for the family to applaud.

At the performances, budding musicians can exercise their powers. An attentive listening is called on to follow the subtlety of the making of live music. This kind of 'being still' will not release itself in the restlessness or hyperactive symptoms which parents have noticed after sessions of TV gazing.

As the reader will see, this book is family-centred. Performances can engage relations and friends, encourage others to do the same, and spread out into the social fabric of the community.

Audrey E McAllen

Introduction

In the first part of this book you will find a description of how the shadow-theatre works and how to make the figures and stage for it. Then all sorts of games with shadows follow.

The second part of the book contains two fairy-tale plays for the shadow-stage with scenery and scenes with figures on them.

Finally there are general hints with useful suggestions and advice.

The idea of this little book is that we don't just sit in front of a ready-made stage, but that we learn to set up everything ourselves.

What is shadow-theatre?

In the evening when the lights are on in the room have you ever conjured up a shadow-show on the wall with your hands?

Hold your hands near the wall, and depending on how you hold them you can see a duck's head, or a rabbit twitching its ears, or a bear opening its mouth wide, on the wall.

Instead of your hands you can take little figures. And instead of the wall you can set up a frame with a screen of thin white paper on it. Then the shadows of your figures appear on the paper.

And if you tell a story as well then you've got a proper shadow-show.

What can we perform on the shadow-stage?

The shadow-theatre always looks a bit magical and mysterious. So it is specially good for doing fairy-tales, sagas and legends. Fairy-tales with ever-recurring snatches or verses which the audience can join in with are very good, like:

Flounder, flounder in the sea,

Come, I pray thee, here to me . . .

But also ghost-stories, adventure stories, and poems about animals and all kinds of odd creatures and fairy-tale beings out of your story-books can come to life on the shadow-stage. You can just conjure up on to this little stage the whole world of wonders and dreams. And you can do it all yourself!

The shadow-stage

For your shadow-theatre first you'll need a stage with a white screen.

You can knock together a very simple shadow-stage out of a deep cardboard box. Cut a square piece out of the middle of the bottom of the box and stick a sheet of thin white paper over the hole from the inside. The paper should be about 2cm (¾") wider than the hole. Put glue on the cardboard round the hole and stick the paper on. Stretch the paper as you stick it on so that it sits taut without any creases. You can also stick the paper behind the window with adhesive tape, in which case it can be easily changed should it get damaged or dirty. Now stand the box on its side and the stage is ready. Put a flat stone or paperweight inside to keep it steady.

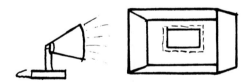

If the show is to be held in the evening, place a small table-lamp behind the stage so that the light falls straight on to the screen.

For making a stage on a table see 'General Hints' page 48.

Cutting out the figures

Cutting out the shadow figures is not difficult. You cut them out of card or black cartridge paper. Take a piece of cartridge paper and just cut into it with your scissors any old way, just as it comes, and suddenly — before you realize — you've got a mushroom or an archway or a manikin. Cut some more figures out. Practice makes perfect! If you think it's easier, draw the figure with a pencil first and then cut it out.

Now try cutting out a person: head, body, arms and legs. Big people, little people, fat and thin ones. They're wearing a dress, a skirt, or trousers, or a coat. Some of them have even got a hat on.

But you must be able to recognize what you've cut out, otherwise you can't recognize the shadow. Test it on the stage.

Animals too are easy to cut out, a dog, a cat, a hedgehog or an elephant. But before you cut out your animals you must draw them with a light coloured crayon to see whether you like them.

Now you're ready to start cutting out figures for a shadow-show. You must cut the profile of the figures because their shadows are then easier to recognize. And you've got to leave a bit of card on the bottom of the figures as a piece to hold them with so that you can move the figures on the stage.

You can read about how to make the figures move, how they sit and walk and dance, in 'General Hints' pages 59–60.

Games
with shadows

Guessing shadows

For this game you don't need to cut out any figures. Instead just collect all sorts of objects which can easily be recognized by their shadows, like a toy fork, a pair of scissors, a comb, a cogwheel, a pencil, even twigs, leaves and flowers.

You lay all these things on the table behind your stage, switch on the light behind the stage and then pass each object across one at a time close behind the screen. The audience will see only the shadow of the object. And they've got to guess by the shadows what the things are which you're showing. I'm sure you'll be able to think up lots more things that will do for this guessing game. Then you'll have lots of new surprises. Of course they can guess at the figures which you've cut out as well. (See page 51).

Here come the musicians

You can set up a song-guessing game for people who like singing or playing instruments. Each person cuts out a picture. There are lots of lovely children's songs which children know and which you can do with only a few figures.

Here are some examples: 'Little Bo-Peep', 'See-saw Marjory Daw', 'Old King Cole', 'Hey diddle diddle the cat and the fiddle', 'Jack and Jill', 'Pussy cat, pussy cat, where have you been?' or the lantern procession song: 'Little lantern, little lantern'.

Once all the pictures have been cut out and you're ready to start, then each person passes one picture after the other slowly across the stage close behind the screen. Then the audience have to guess what song you're showing. The person who guesses right first may sing the song.

The tightrope dancer

Have you ever seen a tightrope dancer, balancing cleverly on a rope? We'll try it on the shadow-stage.

Draw a dancing figure on some black cartridge paper and cut it out. Then stick each end of a piece of thread, about 25 cm (10″) long, on to the arms of the figure so you can make her go along the screen. Wrap the middle of the thread round a piece of cardboard so that you can dangle the figure from above. Now stretch a thin piece of string across behind the stage and fix it tight with adhesive tape to each side. That's the tightrope.

Now let your little dancer go along the rope from one side. Hold her close to the screen to keep the shadow sharp.

Now very carefully and slowly she dances along the rope with little steps and movements. It doesn't matter if she falls off once or twice. That'll make the audience laugh. You see it's not all that easy to get the little figure safely along the rope! But in the end you manage it and you get a hearty applause.

Soft background music suits the play, for example a recorder, a harmonica, a triangle or a lyre.

The enchanted giant

If instead of an electric lamp you use a torch with a small bulb you can conjure up a giant out of a dwarf on your stage. If you hold the figure close to the screen its shadow will be small, just like it's cut out. But as you move it back from the screen its shadow gets bigger and bigger. And you've turned your dwarf into a giant.

You can make a guessing game out of it by starting with a big shadow, with the figure away back from the screen, because sometimes the big shadows look quite different from the figures, and the audience have to do a lot of guessing. Sometimes they don't manage to guess at all and only when you've brought your figure close to the screen can they make out what you're showing.

That's an exciting game. You can take cut-out figures or you can take small suitable objects.

Fishes and wavy tails

This is a game for lots of children. Everyone can cut out a fish. You fold, then cut (see 'General Hints', page 53). In this way you can cut the middle out more easily and you're left with the outside only. After that you stick some grey, black or coloured tissue-paper on the back. For this game hang a sheet of light green tissue-paper behind the screen. Stick it down with adhesive tape at both ends.

When all the fishes are ready stick a handle made of transparent acetate on to each one. With this handle you can get them to swim all over the screen: from above and below and from the side.

The best fish gets a prize, and the others too!

The man on stilts

The man on stilts is an acrobat. He gets on to his high stilts and walks about on them.

He has to have a movable leg so that he can walk properly. You must cut this leg out separately and it's got to be a bit longer than the other, so that you can fix it on to the body with a paper fastener (the kind used to close padded envelopes).

Then the stilts are stuck on to the legs. The stilts should be long enough so that you can use them as handles to move the man across the stage. He can walk forwards and backwards with big steps or little ones just as he fancies.

At the end he can even bow to the audience.

The greedy crocodile

The crocodile can open his mouth wide. His bottom jaw is cut out separately and fixed on to his head with a paper-fastener. Then a piece of wire is fixed to the front of his jaw also with a small paper-fastener. When you push the wire up and down his mouth opens and shuts. (See 'General Hints', page 52.)

The crocodile can now swallow a whole egg and lots of other things. But you've got to practise that a bit, otherwise you might drop the egg. Put a mirror in front of the stage so that you can see how you're getting on.

You'll need two people for this show, one to work the crocodile while the other works the egg and everything else that the croc's going to eat.

Shuddering

For this show you'll need two torches with small bulbs and some sheets of black cartridge-paper. Each sheet must be big enough to cover the whole screen.

Now draw a figure in the middle of each sheet. It can be a witch or a devil or a robber or a dragon with two heads! Then cut the figure out of the black background.

As soon as you've done that the show can start.

Slide the witch's sheet into the grooves for the scenery (See 'General Hints', page 50.)

Switch all the lights off in the room and shine the torches from behind the stage on to the screen. Now the spectators on the other side of the screen can only see the shadow pictures of the witch, but because you are using two sources of light they'll see two witches. And when you move the torches slowly backwards and forwards, up and down, right and left, then the witches' shadows move too. They get long and thin and short and fat, they jump all over the place and do a proper witches' dance.

You can play some suitable music along with it: you can whistle or hum or sing. But softly! The show won't stand too much noise. Then try the same again with different figures, with a devil, a robber or a dragon. Keep on going till everyone has learnt to shudder!

Circus day

This is a good show for a party. Everybody who wants to play cuts out a figure. Once all the figures are cut out the performance can start. One person after the other lets his or her player go across the screen and show his skill.

A gigantic crocodile crawls on and you can see the lions and tigers in their cages.

You can have monkeys too, and they can show how they can climb. They have transparent acetate handles which don't make any shadows.

Then the acrobats appear, the man on stilts, or the funny artist who can balance on a ball. Perhaps there'll be a little tightrope-dancer who is worked by strings from above while someone else holds the rope across the stage.

Last come the two clowns who are going to start a boxing match with enormous boxing-gloves. And don't forget the producer who always makes a deep bow every time he announces the next item on the programme. And the musicians are lined up on one side and sound a fanfare while the drummer thumps the drum.

Two fairy-tale plays

Fundevogel

A fairy-tale play from the Grimm's tale

Players

LINA
FUNDEVOGEL
Sanna, the wicked COOK
THREE SERVANTS
THE ROSE-BUSH with THE ROSE
THE CHURCH with THE CHANDELIER
THE POND
THE DUCK

Stage directions

Cut the COOK out twice, the first figure carrying two pails, the second walking.

Cut LINA out twice as well, once in a nightgown and once in a dress.

Cut out the THREE SERVANTS as one piece.

Going backwards and forwards: Make the figure go out to one side, turn it round, and bring it on again.

Right and left: Always looking from behind the stage.

Scene changes: See 'General Hints', page 60. Scene changes can be made mysterious by playing soft music at the same time, as with the higher notes of a mouth-organ.

The ROSE-BUSH, CHURCH and POND must have

a handle so that they can be brought on and off from the back.

The POND in Scene 5 should be held behind the field, in the middle where the grass is quite short. In the scene change all you have to do is to bring the DUCK and the POND down and then we've got the meadow again.

The *scenery* is cut out in one piece and placed in the scenery-holder (see 'General Hints' page 50). In this way the scenes can be changed quickly.

Curtain: See 'General Hints', page 49.

For directions for cutting out figures see pages 54 to 56.

(The story is read aloud while the characters perform on stage. The first part is read before the stage lights up.)

Once upon a time there was a forester who went to hunt in a wood, and in the wood up in a tree in a nest he found a little child whom he took home with him to his own daughter, Lina, and so the two children grew up together. The boy was called Fundevogel (Bird-foundling) because a bird had carried him off from his mother while she was asleep under a tree. Fundevogel and Lina were so fond of each other that when they could not see each other they were sad.

Scene 1: In front of the house

(The stage lights up. The curtain rises. We can see the house and the fence; the COOK *goes across the stage from right to left and back again carrying two pails.)*

The forester had an old cook, and one evening she took two pails and began to fetch water, and did not go just once but many times out to the well.

(LINA *comes out of the door)*

Lina saw this and said, 'Tell me old Sanna, why are you bringing in so much water?'
'If you will not repeat it to anyone I will tell you.'
Then Lina said 'No,' she would not pass it on to anyone, and the cook said, 'Early tomorrow morning when the forester is out hunting I will boil the water, and when it is seething in the cauldron I will throw Fundevogel in and I will cook him in it.'

(They go into the house. The curtain falls.)

Scene 2: In the bedroom.

(*The curtain rises, we see* LINA *and* FUNDEVOGEL *lying in bed.*)

Next morning very early the forester arose and went hunting, and after he had gone the children were still lying in bed.

Then Lina said to Fundevogel:

'If thou wilt never leave me
I will never leave thee.'

Then Fundevogel said:

'Neither now nor evermore.'

Then said Lina, 'I will just tell you: yesterday evening old Sanna was carrying so many pails of water into the house that I asked her why she was doing that, and she said that if I would not tell anyone she would tell me. I said I would certainly not tell anyone, so she said, next morning when Father would be hunting she would boil up the cauldron full of water, throw you in and cook you. But let us arise quickly and go away together.'

So the two children arose, dressed themselves quickly and went away.

(They get up, move about behind the beds and then run off to the left; the COOK *enters from the right.)*

As soon as the water in the cauldron was boiling the cook went into the bedroom to fetch Fundevogel and throw him in. But when she came in and went to the beds both the children were gone. She grew fearfully afraid and said to herself: 'What shall I say when the forester comes home and sees that the children are gone?'

In her fear she runs hither and thither. 'Quick, after them, that we get them back again.'

(She goes off to the left. The curtain falls.)

Then the cook sent three men servants after them. The servants were to run and catch up with the children.

Scene 3: In the field

(*The curtain rises. We see both children in the field.*)

The children, however, were sitting in front of the forest, and when they saw from afar the three servants coming, Lina said to Fundevogel:
'If thou wilt never leave me
I will never leave thee.'
And Fundevogel said:
'Neither now nor evermore.'
Then said Lina, 'You become the little rose-stem, and I the little rose upon it.'

(*Soft music sounds. The scene changes: the children vanish and a ROSE-BUSH appears with a rose. The THREE SERVANTS come on from the left.*)

When the three servants came to the forest there was nothing there but a rose-bush with a rose on it. but the children were nowhere to be seen. So they said, 'Here is nothing to be done.'

(*They go off to the left. The curtain falls.*)

They went home and told the cook they had seen

35

nothing in the world except a little rose-bush and a rose upon it.

Then the old cook scolded: 'You simple paintbrush-heads, you should have cut the rose-bush in two, broken off the rose and brought it back home. Go and do it quickly!'

So they had to go out for the second time and seek.

Scene 4: In the field

(*The curtain rises.*)

But the children saw them coming from afar and Lina said:

    'Fundevogel, if thou wilt never leave me
    I will never leave thee.'

Fundevogel said:

    'Neither now nor evermore.'

Lina said, 'You become a church and I the chandelier in it.'

(*Soft music sounds. The scene changes: the children vanish and a CHURCH with a chandelier in it appears. The THREE SERVANTS enter.*)

When the three servants came along there was nothing there but a church and a chandelier in it. They said to each other, 'What are we doing here, let us go home.'

(*The curtain falls.*)

Scene 5: In front of the house.

(The curtain rises. The COOK *stands before the door.)*

When the servants came home the cook asked them if they had found anything. They said no, they had not found anything except a church in which there was a chandelier.

'You fools,' scolded the cook, 'Why did you not break down the church and bring the chandelier home?'

Then the old cook set off herself and went after the children with the three servants.

(First the COOK *comes out of the house and walks over the courtyard to the left. She is followed by the* THREE SERVANTS. *The curtain falls.)*

The children saw the three servants coming a long way off and the cook hobbling along behind. Then said Lina:

    'Fundevogel, if thou wilt never leave me
    I will never leave thee.'
And Fundevogel said:
    'Neither now nor evermore.'
Lina said, 'You become the pond and I the duck upon it.'

(Soft music sounds.)

Scene 6: By the pond.

(The curtain rises. We see the POND *and the* DUCK *on it; the* COOK *and the* THREE SERVANTS *come on from the left.)*

The cook came along, and when she saw the pond she lay down leaning over it to drink it all up.

(The COOK *bends down over the water. The* DUCK *comes on from the right towards her.)*

But the duck came swimming along quickly, seized her head in its beak and dragged her into the water. So the old witch was drowned.

(She disappears downwards. Soft music sounds. The scene changes: The POND *and the* DUCK *vanish, and* LINA *and* FUNDEVOGEL *appear again beside each other.)*

The children went home together and were very happy; and if they have not died they are still alive.

(Both go off slowly to the left, accompanied by music. The curtain falls.)

Little jugful

A Norwegian fairy tale

Players:

THE LITTLE HOUSE
THE GIRL
THE LITTLE JUG
THE MOUSE
THE FARMER

Stage directions

The little HOUSE should be partly off the screen to the left so that you can hold it and waggle it when it dances with joy. Cut it out separately and put it behind the patch of grass in the scenery groove.

The chimney smokes. Cut out a long wavy piece of grey or blue acetate or cellophane, narrower than the chimney, and move it up and down above the chimney from behind. The chimney is smoking.

The little JUG must be quite big so that a lot can go into it. Cut out four jugs, one empty, one full of meat, one with honey-buns and the fourth with coins. Make each handle for you to move the jug out of transparent acetate.

The little jug runs. Accompany with little noises or music so that the audience can hear it coming. You can take strips of wood laid on something soft, and lightly drum a pencil on them.

The jug breaks. Let it roll down the steps and take it away below.

The MOUSE does not peep out of the can. It is hiding! Its handle is also made of acetate so that it can't be seen when the mouse jumps out of the house.

You can elaborate this shadow-play even further by making extra scenes for when the jug is at the butcher's, the baker's, in the inn and at the market.

You will need a whole troupe of players! For instructions on cutting out the figures, see page 57.

Scene 1

(The stage lights up, on the left we see a little house with steps in front. The story is read aloud.)

Once upon a time there was a little house. It looked a poor little house, all blown squint and wobbly. In it lived a girl who had spent her last farthing and had used everything up. Now she had nothing left; only one single little jug. But the jug was empty.

The girl had washed the little jug quite clean, rinsed it out, and put it in front of the door to dry in the sun.

(*The* GIRL *puts the* JUG *out.*)

And suddenly, what do you think, the jug began to run, down the steps, helter-skelter, and along the road.

(*The* JUG *runs off to the right.*)

And where do you think the little jug was off to, so clean and washed? I will tell you. It went running off to the butcher's. There the butcher's boy was cutting up meat on the table for soup. That is where the little jug went.

(*It can be heard coming back.*)

Listen, there it is coming back.

(*The* JUG *comes from the right.*)

But look it is not empty any more. There is some-thing in it! It climbs up the steps and knocks on the door. The girl hears the knocking and calls:

GIRL (*calls from within*): Who's out there?
JUG: Little jugful.
GIRL (*comes out of the house*): Little jug what have you got for me?
JUG: Look in my tummy and see!
GIRL (*looks in*): Meat for soup, and ham! Who gave you that?

41

JUG: From the table it fell, and I caught it so well.
GIRL: What a good little jug you are, come right in and we'll cook it.

(*Both go into the house.*)

And the girl took the meat straight out of the jug and cooked it, and stewed it, and the poor little house began to dance with joy and the smoke went puffing thick out of the chimney.

(*The little* HOUSE *dances up and down and smoke comes out of the chimney. Slowly it grows dark.*)

Scene 2

(*The stage lights up again; and the little jug is standing on the step.*)

Next morning again the girl washed her little jug and rinsed it out till it was shining clean, and set it on the step to dry. And what do you suppose? The little pot began to run again. It sprang down the steps helter-skelter and ran along the road.

(*The JUG goes off to the right.*)

Do you know where it went to this time? To the baker's. There the baker's boy was heaping up the fresh honey-buns on to the table. That is where the little jug went. Look, now, it's just coming back.

(*The JUG comes from the right.*)

There it is. Once again it has brought something. Now it is knocking at the door.

GIRL (*calls from within*): Who's out there?
JUG: Little jugful.
GIRL (*comes out of the house*): Little jug, what have you got for me?
JUG: Look in my tummy and see!
GIRL: Honey-buns! The whole jug full! Who gave you that?
JUG: From the table it fell, and I caught it so well.
GIRL: What a good little jug you are, come right in and we'll eat them up.

(*Both go into the house.*)

The girl took the honey-buns out of the jug, made some nice sweet milk and then she licked and munched so that the poor little house again began to dance with joy and the smoke went puffing thick out of the chimney.

(*The* HOUSE *dances up and down and smoke comes out of the chimney. The stage grows dark.*)

Scene 3

(*The stage lights up: we see the house again and the* JUG *is on the steps.*)

The poor girl was very happy now. Next morning very early she washed the jug nice and clean, rinsed it out and put it out on the step to dry. And again it began to run. It sprang down the steps helter-skelter, and ran along the road.

(*The* JUG *goes out to the right.*)

Where is it going this time? I know. It is going to the inn. There the farmers are sitting at table and counting out their money. That is where the little jug goes. And it is not long before it comes back, clinkety-clank, clinkety-clank, clinkety-clank, clonk up against the door.

(*The* JUG *comes from the right and goes up to the house.*)

GIRL (*calls from within*): Who's out there?
JUG: Little jugful.
GIRL (*comes out of the house*): Little jug, what have you got for me?
JUG: Look in my tummy and see!
GIRL (*looks in*): Beautiful silver crowns! Who gave them to you?
JUG: From the table they fell, and I caught them so well.
GIRL: What a good little jug you are, come right in and we shall count them.

(*Both go into the house.*)

The girl picked up the jug right away and emptied all the money out, and she turned the silver crowns over and over so that once again the poor little house began to dance with joy and the last smoke went puffing thick out of the chimney.

(*The* HOUSE *dances, the chimney smokes, then everything stands still.*)

Now you can well imagine how glad the girl was. But she wanted more! And because she grew so greedy she thought: 'Why should I wait till tomorrow before I send off the jug? It ought to bring me something else today.' So she did not wash the jug, she did not rinse it; no, she just put it out on the step right away.

(*The* GIRL *pushes the* JUG *out.*)

And really and truly the jug began to run! It sprang down the steps helter-skelter and ran along the road till it came to the market-place.

(*The* JUG *goes off to the right.*)

There it stopped. The market had just finished, and the mice had gathered up all that was left. Now a little mouse crept into the jug to have a cosy sleep. As soon as the little jug noticed that it crept home very, very softly.

(*The* JUG *comes from the right, creeps slowly towards the house, and knocks on the door.*)

GIRL (*calls from within*): Who's out there?
JUG: Little jugful.
GIRL (*comes out of the house*): What a good little jug you are, come right in.

(*They both go into the house.*)

What will be in the jug this time, wondered the girl, and she put her hand inquisitively into the jug. And out jumped the mouse.

(*The* MOUSE *jumps out of the house and off to the right.*)

'Oh, you bad little jug!' cried the girl, and she was so angry that she hurled the jug out of the door.

(*The* JUG *rolls out and stops rolling.*)

And now the jug was all broken.

When the girl came out of the house and saw that the jug was broken she began to cry, 'What a poor girl am I, what shall I do now?'

(*A* FARMER *comes from the left and stands behind her.*)

By good fortune along came a farmer and said to her, 'Come with me to my farm. There you can milk the cows.'
The girl went with the farmer to his farm, milked the cows and was content.

(*Both go off together to the right; it grows dark.*)

General hints

Building a stage

Stage

If several children all want to do the play at the same time you can make a bigger folding stage out of cardboard or hardboard. It has three pieces: the front and two side pieces. In the middle of the front piece cut or saw out the opening and stick a sheet of white paper over it from the back, just like the small cardboard stage.

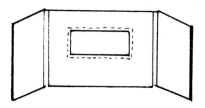

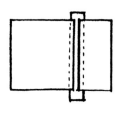

Tape the wings on to the middle piece, one on the right, the other on the left. To stick the panels together lay the panels with the outer sides uppermost on the table, leaving a gap of 5 mm (¼") between the boards, and stick a strip of wide adhesive tape along the edge, leaving about 2 cm (1") sticking out at each end. Fold these ends of adhesive tape over and stick them down on the other side of the cardboard. Turn the cardboad over. Take a fresh strip of adhesive tape the same length as the height of the panels and stick it along the edges so that it covers the turned over pieces. Now the sheets are joined and they can be folded if needed.

Lighting

For night scenes you can drape a thin cloth over your lamp. In this way you can get a mysterious and magical lighting.

Curtain

Once you've made your little cardboard stage you can use the other half of the cardboard box as a curtain. Cut off the side pieces and put the middle bit in front of the stage. That's the curtain down.

If you've built a bigger stage out of hardboard or plywood you can put on a proper curtain. Screw in two eye-screws above the screen, one to the left and the other to the right. Stretch a curtain-wire or string from one eye to the other and you can hang a little curtain on with little rings. The curtain is always made up of two pieces.

And if you're good at making things you can make it so that it can be drawn.

The curtain must be made of thick stuff so that no one can see through it.

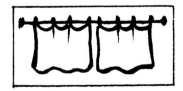

Scenery

Sometimes you need scenery for your shadow-show: a tree, a wooden fence, or a house. To hold the scenery behind the stage you need a strip of cardboard fixed below the screen. But only stick it along the bottom. Leave the upper edge free. You can then insert the pieces of scenery. Or you can fix the scenery with adhesive tape, and afterwards you can take the strip of tape off again.

Making the figures

Cutting out

Don't move the scissors round when you're cutting.
Just move the paper round and round. To start with
you can draw your figures with a pencil and then cut
them out. Later on try and cut them out free-hand.
The figures will then be more alive! Don't give your
figures thin legs, otherwise they will tip over. A boy
is best in long trousers and a princess with a wide
flared out dress reaching right down to her feet.

Leave a strip of paper below the feet as a handle,
so that you can move the figures without your hands
appearing on the stage.

Figures

The figures you cut out don't always have to look
like real people. You can make quite magical figures
like trolls and leprechauns, giants and dwarfs,
witches and monsters and lots of other things. The
shadow-theatre is like a fairy-tale: in it there are all
sorts of shapes and forms.

Figure-holders

You can make figure-holders out of matchboxes.
Place the box on its end. Insert the handle of the
figure into the slot at the end of the lid. The figure
will now stand and you can move it about.

Figures with movable parts

You can cut the bigger animal figures out of card and make them with movable parts. For that you need a paper-punch, a bradawl or pointed scissors to make the holes, then large and small paper fasteners (the kind used for fastening padded envelopes) and strong transparent acetate. And this is how it's done:

If you want to have a movable arm, cut the figure out without an arm and then cut the arm out separately. The arm should be cut longer at the top so that it fits over the shoulder.

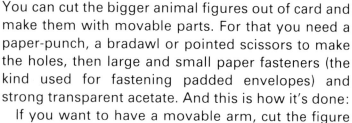

Now you can make holes through the shoulder and the top of the arm and fix a paper-fastener through both holes. Bend out the fastener behind and cover with sellotape.

Now the figure has got a movable arm. We still need a handle so that we can move the arm. You can make this handle with wire, but if you can get thick acetate that is better, for then the spectators won't be able to see the lever. Fix the lever to the centre of the arm by making two holes, one in the arm and one in the lever and push a paper-fastener through them both.

Now we can move the arm with the handle from below. You can try the same for a movable head or leg.

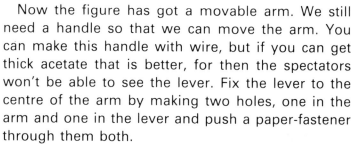

Fishes

The fishes are cut out from a folded paper. First draw a fish on stiff black cartridge paper. Then fold it in half lengthwise and cut it out. Next cut the inside of the fish out so that only the outer edge is left. Unfold the fish and stick it on to grey, black or coloured tissue-paper. From the extra tissue paper sticking out from the outline of the fish you can cut the fins and tail. Stick on a round eye.

Stick a piece of transparent acetate on to the edge of the fish as a handle, so that you can move the fish about behind the screen. If you want a coloured background hang a sheet of coloured tracing paper (for instance, light green) behind the screen, fixing it with adhesive tape at the sides of the stage.

Handles

For birds and figures that come down on to the stage from above we can also use handles made of transparent acetate film. Stick them on to the figures. The spectator can't see these handles. You can buy acetate film in an art shop or good stationers. If the acetate is too thin stick two pieces together with transparent adhesive.

Black cartridge paper

This can also be bought in an art shop or good stationers.

Figures for copying and cutting out

If you can draw you can think up your own figures for your shadow-theatre. They'll be much more alive then and look just like what you yourself imagined.

For others who might find that a bit difficult here are some figures which belong to the two plays in this book.

Sanna, the cook   *One of the three servants*

Fundevogel

Lina

Sanna with water buckets

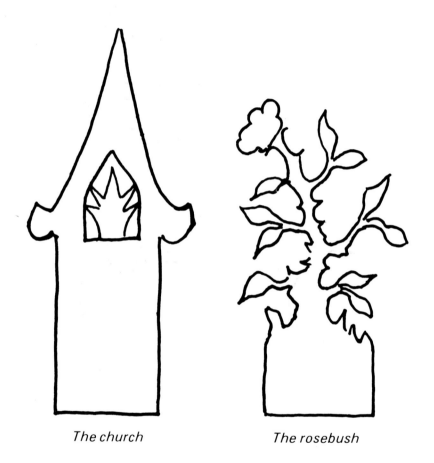

The church   *The rosebush*

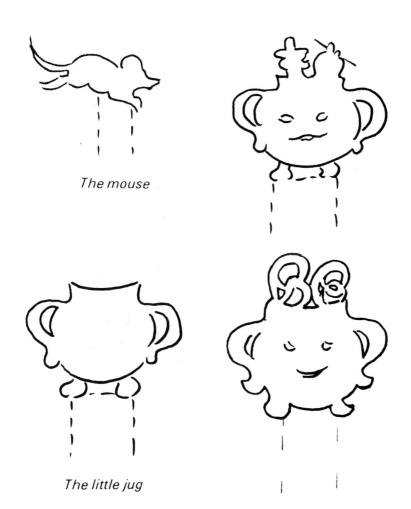

The mouse

The little jug

The farmer   The girl

Putting on a production

Tidiness

This is very important, especially behind the stage. Otherwise you can land up not finding a figure that you need for going on next. It's best to lay out all the figures going on stage in a row on the table behind the stage.

Rehearsal

Of course you'll have a rehearsal or two before you perform your play, because you'll want the audience to be pleased with it. When you rehearse place a mirror in front of your stage, then you can watch your own playing.

Coming on

Move the figures along close to the screen behind the stage so that their shadows fall sharply on to the screen. The figure must come on from the side and go off again to the side. But you can bring off witches, giants and other magical beings by bringing them back towards you. Then the shadows grow bigger and bigger until the shape has vanished.

Turning round

If a figure has to be turned round during the play don't do it on the open stage, but bring it off to the side, turn it round quickly and bring it on again. You can also turn figures round behind a house or a tree.

Moving the figures

There are figures with moving parts, and those that don't have moving parts. Let's start with those that haven't got moving parts: they're easier to make. Even these can look alive if you work them properly.

Supposing the figure is meant to walk, make it do little sideways movements so that it doesn't just glide along.

If it's a rather proud figure lean him a bit backwards — nose in the air. To make the figure bow, push him over forwards.

You can even make your figures dance! Move them about a bit, up and down, left and right. You can also make them dance by holding them from above by a thread. Stick the ends of the thread on to the arms. If your stage is too small, turn it round and do the play from the other side.

Changing scenes

In the shadow-theatre you can make a figure disappear and change it into another in the open. Then you don't take the figure off to the side but towards the back. Then the shadow gets bigger and bigger

which makes the transformation even more
mysterious. And the new figure comes on in the
same way.

Production

If you want to perform a shadow-play of a fairy-tale
or a story, you don't need to write a play for it; you
simply tell the story or read it, and the bits of the
story which suit the play best you can perform with
your figures.

What's best is if you've got an assistant who reads
out the story while you are working the figures. Of
course you can perform a shadow-play all by yourself
but then you must know your story off by heart,
because it won't work if you try to read the story
from a book and work the figures at the same time.

Music

Music belongs to the shadow-theatre. But it must be
soft. The shadow theatre won't stand any loud noise;
for the shadows that we see are like dreams, you
can't hold on to them. Suitable instruments are
recorder, mouth-organ, little chimes, triangle and the
lyre. Glass dishes and wine glasses have a lovely
sound when placed on a soft mat and carefully struck
with a pencil.

Sunnhild Reinckens

Making Dolls

This little book with its many colour photographs and simple diagrams describes how to make seventeen different kinds of doll: a cuddly doll for toddlers, a large baby doll, finger puppets, gnomes, dolls for a doll's house, and many others. There are clear instructions on how to form the head, make the body, create different hair-styles, and indicate the features of the face.

Sunnhild Reinckens lives in Hanover, West Germany. She holds doll-making courses for children, mothers, fathers and grandparents. She believes it is better that people make a simple doll, however modest, than buy one in the shop for their children.

Freya Jaffke

Toymaking with Children

The toys surrounding a child during his first five years are of great importance. They awaken the imagination and stimulate creativity. Out of her long experience as a kindergarten teacher Freya Jaffke makes numerous suggestions for making toys and from wooden boats, log trains and doll's furniture to rag dolls, puppets and soft animals.

This is an excellent handbook abounding with ideas for parents of young children.

Floris Books

Thomas Berger

The Christmas Craft Book

Simply made decorations for home or school are an absorbing way for children to become involved in the celebration of Advent and Christmas. Over the years Thomas Berger and his family have perfected the decorations included here.

Parents, teachers and children will quickly learn to make crib figures, candles, lanterns, angels and a variety of Christmas tree decorations which are all described and fully illustrated in colour photographs.

M van Leeuwen and J Moeskops

The Nature Corner

Seasonal nature tables are an invaluable way of making young children aware of the changing cycle of the year. With simple materials and basic knitting and crocheting skills a series of colourful and effective tableaux can be made at home or in school for depicting the seasons and major festivals.

Instructions and diagrams are provided for making the figures and objects, along with basic hints for setting up the table and involving children in creating the whole. Each of the eleven tableaux is illustrated in full colour.

Floris Books

Walter Kraul

Earth, Water, Fire and Air
Playful explorations in the four elements

This craft book for children shows how to make a waterwheel, paddle-steamer, propeller plane, parachute, windmill, simple pendulum clock, spinning tops, a little hot-air carousel or roundabout, a hot-air balloon, and lots more.

Some suggestions are simple enough for six-year-olds, others challenging enough for a skilful twelve-year-old.

Brunhild Müller

Painting with Children

A vital factor in a child's development is the stimulation of active imagination and creativity. Müller suggests ideas for encouraging self-expression from children through watercolour painting, and attempts to understand their fantasies.

Floris Books